Transform Your Habit Transform Your Life

Be the Person You Were ALWAYS Meant To Be

John. S. Lawson

DEDICATION

This Book Is Dedicated To All Who Wants To Break Free From The Shackles Of Ineffective Habits. Because You Deserve To Live Productively And Happily.

&

I dedicate this book as well to my two beautiful children and my loving wife who have been nothing short of being my light and joy throughout the years.

CONTENTS

INTRODUCTION

Congratulations on purchasing the book Transform Your Habit, Transform Your Life: Because you Deserve to Live a Better Life.

In this book, you will find tips and tricks on how to kick those bad habits and live a more fulfilling life. Bad habits are a natural thing. Everybody has to deal with them at some point in their life. Even the most powerful person in the world has a habit they want to kick. In this book, you will discover what could be causing your problems, and a way to help you move past them.

Everybody is different, so what may work for one person may not work for you. Keep this in mind as you move forward. This won't be a miracle cure, and it won't happen overnight. It will also take some work to change your habits for good. The more you put into to changing, the more of a payoff you will get. Some patterns are caused by severe disorders such as OCD or PTSD. If you feel this could be you, then please confer with a medical professional.

It's a fact that at some point in your life there will be something you want to change about yourself. It may be that you want to lose a couple of pounds, or cut back on your drinking, or improve your sleeping habits. It won't be easy either. Nothing in life ever is. I'm here to help you. I will guide you step by step through the process.

Throughout this book, you will learn what causes your bad habits, why it's so hard to kick them, and how to overcome them. It may seem impossible to change. You have a lot on your plate. You work, you have children to take care of, you go to school, what have you. It's stressful. I know, but you're not alone. There are simple adjustments that can be made throughout your hectic day, and before you know it things will start to change.

CHAPTER ONE

A WARNING

Everybody is different, making every habit different. That means that all these tips coming up are subjective. It's not something that will work for everybody. Another thing you need to be aware of is that your habit could be something more. I'm going to go over this possible problem quickly. Keep in mind this is not to cure or diagnose you with anything. If you think you may have a psychological disorder, as opposed to a bad habit, please seek medical attention.

For your information, a habit is defined as a settled or regular tendency or practice; especially one that is hard to give up.

OCD, obsessive compulsive disorder, can be confused as a habit. OCD can fall into four main categories;

- checking

- contamination/mental contamination

- hoarding

- ruminations/intrusive thoughts

OCD is diagnosed by when obsessions and compulsions:

- Consume excessive amounts of time

- Causes significant distress

- Interferes with daily functions

Your habit, itself, could be OCD, or your inability to break the habit, could be caused by OCD. An example of OCD being the habit would be hoarding. An example of OCD interfering your ability to break a habit would be intrusive thoughts. Now, when breaking a habit you will have intrusive thoughts, but they should just come and go. If your intrusive thoughts are constant and interfere with your life, then OCD could be a factor.

Other psychological disorders that could be confused with a habit are, eating disorders. Anorexia nervosa and bulimia nervosa are common eating disorders where people end up starving themselves or binging and purging. A lesser known eating disorder, which is the one most likely to be confused as a habit, is a binge-eating disorder.

With binge-eating disorder, people lose control of their eating habits. Unlike with bulimia nervosa, periods of binges are not followed by purging, which is why most people with binge-eating disorder are overweight. It is the top eating disorder in the US. Symptoms of binge-eating disorder are:

- Eating an unusually large amount of food in a specific amount of time

- Eating even when you're full or not hungry

- Eating fast during binge episodes

- Eating until you are uncomfortably full

- Eating alone or in secret to avoid embarrassment

- Feeling distressed, ashamed, or guilty when not eating

- Frequent dieting, possibly without weight loss

Chances are everybody can say that they have experienced one or more of these symptoms. For example, most holidays' people will over eat. That does not mean you have binge-eating disorder. Keep in mind disorders interrupt your everyday life, and happen constantly. If you just overeat when watching TV, or when you're bored, then you probably don't have a disorder. If you are concerned that you might, then please seek medical advice.

Make sure that if you think you have a disorder to see your doctor make sure. It's better to believe you have a disease than go around with an undiagnosed disorder. I want to make sure that you can live the life you deserve and making sure that your habit isn't something more serious is important.

CHAPTER TWO

A HISTORY OF HABITS

Imagine this; your alarm goes off. You slide out of bed and slump your way to the bathroom. You do your business and then hop in the shower. Once finished you brush your teeth before you get dressed. Once dressed you head to the kitchen to have your coffee and breakfast. Now, what just happened? You were on complete autopilot. You are so used to doing the same thing every morning you don't have to think about it. That is what a habit is.

Human beings are creatures of habit. We get into a routine, and we stick to it. Then it becomes a struggle to change.

Chances are your habits are caused by stress or boredom. You start doing things to distract your brain from the stress or boredom, giving you brain a brief moment of utopia.

Stress and boredom aren't just triggers for certain habits. They're triggers for most habits. Whether you have a problem with eating, smoking, biting your nails, or spending mindless hours on the computer, whatever it may be you're using the habit to suppress those emotions. There is a chance that a deeper issue causes the stress or boredom that is being felt.

Ask yourself, is there a belief or a reason you're holding onto this habit?

The key to overcoming a habit is to figure out what is causing it. Did something happen when you were younger? Do you believe something bad is going to happen if you stop?

That's why there is no one solution. Take the habit of smoking. According to the World Health Organization, more than one billion people smoke. Most of those people are smoking for different reasons. Some may smoke because they saw their parents smoke, or their friends. They may have started smoking as a way to cope with stress.

A Loop

Every habit begins with a psychological pattern. The habit loop is a three-part process. It begins with a trigger. The trigger tells you brain to go into automatic mode and let a behavior happen. The second part is the routine which is the actual habit itself. The last part is the reward. The reward is something your brain likes and helps it remember the loop in the future.

According to neuroscientists, habit-making behaviors are controlled in the basal ganglia. The basal ganglia are also the area of the brain that controls emotions, memories, and patterns. As stated above, a habit is a pattern.

Decisions are controlled in the prefrontal cortex. A habit starts as a behavior or decision, but the more you do it, the less the brain works. The decision-making part of your brain goes to sleep. That's what makes multitasking possible.

Good habits are programmed the same as bad habits are. A good habit, such as brushing your teeth, gets programmed by repetition just like smoking. Or learning to parallel park works the same as overeating.

The fact that they work the same is a good thing.

That makes it easier for you to retrain your brain.

Problems

There are going to be problems when trying to break a habit, especially if your habit involves any stimulant. At that point, you're not just trying to stop the habit, but also working through the detox symptoms. For example, nicotine, via tobacco, is one of the most heavily consumed drugs in the world. In Australia, smoking is one of the biggest causes of, preventable, death, killing about 15,000 people per year. It's also one of the hardest to quit. Withdrawal from nicotine can cause insomnia, irritability, anxiety, and difficulty concentrating.

Slip-ups are inevitable, but if you're working to break a habit that involves any stimulating drug, it's going to be a lot harder. This could include smoking, drinking, even coffee. Keep this in the back of your mind so that you are prepared.

John. S. Lawson

CHAPTER THREE

A HABITS HABITAT

Necessarily true. You can control your habits, but your environment plays a huge part of what you do on a daily basis. One of your brain's primary functions is to find and use patterns as shortcuts to process the information we're presented with on a daily basis.

In a study conducted on habits vs. intentions, researchers found that students that switched Universities were more likely to change their daily habits. Those habits were easier to change than they were for the control group because they weren't exposed to familiar daily cues. This can be seen in every bad habit that somebody has.

Eating Habits

Have you ever been driving home from work, not thinking about food, when you see your favorite fast food joint, and suddenly your start craving a cheeseburger? It's not your fault. Everybody experiences moments like that.

Our food environment is broken down into two categories; the atmosphere we encounter when eating, and how food is portioned. The cues vary from what's being eaten, its packaging or utensil size, and the amount of food. Think about when you eat out. You will undoubtedly receive a huge plate of food. You don't think you can eat it all, but then you end up cleaning your plate. Seeing an empty plate signals satiety in our brains.

Maybe eating at home will help you avoid these

triggers. Not so fast. Home plate sizes have increased 22% over the last century. Where you store your food also plays a large part in your eating habits, bringing new meaning to "Out of sight, out of mind."

Don't worry though. There are ways to overcome these triggers.

- First, choose smaller plates to use at home. It takes less food to fill up a small plate. You're eating less, but you're still cleaning your plate and making your brain happy.

- Another way is to pre-portion your food. Have everything portioned out into single servings.

- It also helps to focus on one thing at a time. When you're eating, only concentrate on eating. Try not to watch TV or the computer while you're eating.

- Most importantly learn the true signs of hunger and avoid mindless eating. This comes in handy when you're not in control of the food.

Smoking Habits

Environmental triggers for smokers can be harder to break than triggers for overeaters. According to the American Psychological Association is in an area associated with smoking can cause a smoker to have a craving. That means they could walk into a bar where there are no cigarettes, ashtrays, or other smokers, yet still, have a craving because they associate the setting with smoking.

Your regular daily routine could also cause triggers. Some people associate their morning cup of coffee with smoking. An easy fix for that is to keep yourself busy in the morning. Try to distract yourself from the craving. You can also trade your coffee out for tea or juice.

Most smokers smoke while driving making the car another common trigger. If you have cravings whenever you drive try singing along to the radio or a CD. You could also substitute smoking with chewing gum while driving.

Stress is another major trigger for smokers. Cigarettes have thousands of chemicals in them that trick your brain into thinking that they are helping relieve your stress. The key to overcoming the stress trigger is to find new ways to relieve your stress. Meditation and yoga are both good stress management techniques.

Drinking Habits

Stress and anxiety are big triggers for drinking. As I mentioned earlier, they are also the cause for most habits.

There are two main types of triggers; external and internal. External are people, places, or things that trigger you desire to drink. They are easier to avoid than internal triggers. Internal triggers are, as the name states, inner emotions that trigger your desire to drink.

A good way to figure out exactly what causes your triggers is to track them for a week. Keep a journal with you and every time you have the urge to drink, write down what happened or where you were that caused the urge.

Some simple ways to avoid external triggers are to keep little, to no alcohol, at home. Socially, try avoiding situations that involve drinking. You may feel guilty turning down invitations to go out with your friends, but just remember it's not forever. You only have to turn them down until your urges become more manageable.

It won't be possible to stay away from all triggers. Always remind yourself why you are making this change. Keep a list somewhere on your person that you can read when you have the urge to drink. Talk to an accountability partner. That's what they're there for. Distract yourself. Find something to do to keep your mind off your urge. Lastly, you could also ride it out. Problem the hardest, but tell yourself that it's only temporary. That the feeling will pass.

Using your Triggers

You can also use your triggers for good. Task association is a good way to control your triggers. For instance, doctors have helped insomniacs by telling them to only go to bed when they are sleepy. If they can't sleep, they are told to go to a different room that way their bed is only associated with sleep. This could work to cut back on environmental triggers.

Instead of keeping snacks close to your work area, keep them in the kitchen or break room. That way you associate your desk with working and not with eating. Train yourself to associate your car with singing along with the radio instead of smoking. Only eat at the kitchen table and not on the couch. That way the couch is only for watching TV and the kitchen table is for eating.

CHAPTER FOUR

A SIMPLE BREAK

I'm going to start with the most basic three steps of breaking a bad habit. I don't want to overload you with a bunch of information. These first three basic steps will give you the building blocks to move onto more in-depth information.

The first step you have to take in breaking a habit is the decision to break the habit. You're probably thinking, "Duh," but you have to make sure you have a reason. If you don't have a reason to quit, you will not quit. You won't get anywhere if you go at this thinking you "might" have something you need to change. You have to know and want to change. Make a list of the reasons why you want to stop. If you can't think of anything, make a list of the bad things that will happen if you don't stop. For example, if you don't stop binge eating you could become overweight and develop serious health problems.

The next step is to be ready to face your boredom or emotions. As mentioned before habits are formed out of boredom or stress. You have to be willing to take a look at your life and figure out how to change what is causing your dissatisfaction. You must be ready to face the discomfort. We as humans don't like discomfort, but if you can overcome that, then you have surpassed one of the biggest hurdles. Make your life the way you want it to be.

The last step is to find a new way to relieve stress. You could have the life of your dreams, but you still suffer from stress. You feel stressed, so you turn to alcohol. You drink, and then you don't feel stressed. That makes you think you have everything together. Instead, you need to replace you drinking with something new, something healthy. You could use meditation or exercise as a healthy alternative.

The first three steps are:

1. Make sure you have a good reason to break your habit

2. Be ready to face the emotions and boredom that is causing your habit

3. Find a new way to handle your stress

Starting with these three steps will put you well on your way to breaking your bad habit. In the coming chapters, I will go into more detail on how to switch out your bad habits for new healthy habits.

A Big Break

As learned in the last chapter, there are three necessary steps to breaking habits. While those three steps are paramount there are other tips and tricks to take your habit breaking to the next level. We'll discuss several of them in this chapter, and flesh out even more throughout the rest of the book. A big part of break a bad habit is replacing it with a new one; I'll wait until later to explain how to start said new habit. Now, let's look at some tips to kick those habits to the curb.

1. Set a Start Date

Mark it on your calendar when you want to start changing your habit. You have to be serious about this, so having a countdown will help you to stay on track. The countdown will help to create excitement. Just like a child counting down the 25 to Christmas, or the days before their birthday. You want to drastically change your life for the better, so there should be an element of excitement.

2. Bait and Switch

Once you know what habit you want to change then, you can sub a new habit, temporary or permanent, in its place. If you're a nail-biter, try subbing in gum. Gum can also be used to help with smoking urges.

3. Discover your triggers

Knowing why we make certain decisions is the key to conquering your habits. Often we perform the habit without even realizing we're doing it. That's why it's called a habit. For a long time after my Dad quit smoking, every time he got in the car he would roll down the window and fiddle with his pocket because that's what he would do when he smoked. He never even realized he was doing that until we told him. But you can fix that by being consciously aware of when you perform your habit. There are five main triggers for habits; location, time, emotional state, other people, and an immediately preceding action. Start to take notes whenever you perform the bad habit. Soon you will be able to figure out what is triggering your problem.

4. Don't go cold turkey

Everybody has probably tried to give up something cold turkey. Cold turkey is a favorite of smokers, but it rarely ever works. It's similar to telling a child to not do something, and that will be exactly what they go and do. Cold turkey is centered on perfection. People think that they if they slip up then they have failed. Nobody is perfect. Cold Turkey leaves no wiggle room, and with something like this, you need a little wiggle room.

5. Switch up your environment

You don't have to move or do anything drastic. The smallest change can switch your brain's thinking. You always smoke in the parking lot at work; the parking lot becomes a trigger. If you change your routine just slightly you will trick your brain into not craving a cigarette. You can also use the 20-second rule. Make it so that it takes 20 more seconds for you to make your habit. If you smoke, keep your cigarettes in a draw where you have to walk to get them. If you have a problem with snacking, put your snacks in the back of the pantry.

6. Make it incremental

The best way to make a change is to set daily

incremental changes. You need to wean yourself off of you habit. The first step is to establish a baseline. This is going to differ according to what you want to change. Such as; how much time you watch TV, how many cigarettes you smoke each day, how many drinks you consume when out with friends. Then choose how much you're going to give up each week. If you're a smoker and you typically smoke a whole pack a day; then the first week or two you go to 15. Then the next two weeks you go down to 10, and so on until you stop smoking.

7. Don't focus on what you don't want

Most everybody that makes a goal will make this mistake. They will say, I'm not going to do this, or I'm not going to that. Setting a goal like that is setting you up for failure. Instead, decide what you are going to do. It's similar to the bait and switch. If you know you like to snack when working; instead of saying you're not going to snack, say you are going to snack on vegetables. Then all you have to do is switch your chips out for carrots.

8. Do it in honor of yourself

Research shows that people that try to break habits out of frustration or guilt will ultimately fail. People that respect themselves and are happy with who they are will be more successful. Work to change your bad habit from a position of personal strength and confidence.

9. Make a declaration

Social media has become a big part of most everybody's day. Use this to your advantage. Announce on social media the change you are going to make if you feel comfortable doing so. Then keep them updated as you progress. Chances are you will have friends that will congratulate you, and that will make you feel good about what you are doing. This one, of course, isn't for everybody. Some habits that you are trying to break may not be something you want to share with the whole world. Some habits are very personal, so if you don't feel comfortable sharing it with a large group of people, then you don't have to. Keep in mind though having somebody to talk to can help you along the way.

10. Be prepared to forgive yourself

There will be slip-ups. We are only human beings, and we learn from out slip ups. When you slip up, forgive yourself. Wake up the next day ready to beat your habit. Don't go at it with an all or nothing attitude. There are no scorecards in life. The slip up happened, learn from it, and move on. If you are serious about beating this habit, you won't throw your hands up in defeat after a few lapses.

Classical Conditioning

Classical conditioning is a psychological learning process that occurs when two stimuli are repeatedly paired; a response that is at first elicited by the second stimulus is eventually elicited by the first stimulus alone. An example of this is Pavlov's dog.

Pavlov trained his dog to associate the thrill of being fed with the sound of a bell. He would ring a bell every time he gave the dogs their food. After several repeats of this the dog associated the sound of the bell with receiving food. The dogs would then begin to salivate every time they heard the bell.

This theory doesn't just apply to salivating dogs. Over the years it has formed an important rationale for the development, maintenance, and a relapse of bad habits.

Habits work much in the same way as Pavlov's dogs did. For a smoker, just the site of a pack of cigarettes will elicit a dopamine response causing them to have the urge to smoke. This isn't restricted to smokers either. The same dopamine response happens in alcoholics, overeaters, and so on.

This can be used in reverse, to break a habit. The bell was the trigger for the dogs to start salivating because they knew the food was coming. Just like if a smoker always lights up when they get in the car. The car is the trigger for the smoker to want to smoke. If you start ringing the bell for the dog but don't give them food they will eventually learn that the bell no longer means food. If you stop lighting up every time you get in the car eventually you won't have that trigger anymore.

This is definitely one of the more complicated and harder ways of breaking a habit, but it will work. All the rest have ways of distracting your brain, making it easier to change.

Procrastination

Everybody has been faced with procrastination at some point. It can also be detrimental in your ability to break a habit. But just like breaking a habit, you can overcome procrastination.

In a nutshell, procrastination is when you continually put off doing something. The first step, like with most things, is **realizing you are procrastinating**. If you're honest with yourself, then you know when you are procrastinating, but if you're not sure here are some ways to know;

- Waiting for the right mood, or day to start something

- Doing unimportant tasks to avoid what you need to be doing

- Sitting down to start working, then immediately going to do something else

Once you've realized you are procrastinating, then

you can move onto the next step.

Figure out why you are procrastinating. It could be either you or the task. You might find the task unpleasant. Which, since you're changing a habit, you probably will find the task unpleasant. You could also be disorganized or overwhelmed. An important part of the habit breaking process is being organized and knowing what you are doing. Another reason could be that your heart is not into it. You don't have a good enough reason to change this habit.

Lastly, **adopt anti-procrastination strategies**. Procrastination itself is a habit. As you've learned, the only way of getting rid of a habit is persistently not doing the habit. The same tricks you have or will learn about breaking a habit will work to keep you from procrastination. Set up a reward system. Have somebody check in with you. Anything that will keep you accountable in some way, shape, or form.

Be Prepared

Unfortunately, a fact of the world is there will be people that want to sabotage you and your goals. It's not bad enough that you will have self-Sabotaging moments, but you will have to handle other people trying to do the same thing. You have to be prepared to ignore them. They may or may not know what they're doing. Their words can be poison to your success. The moment you start taking their words of "advice" will be your first steps towards failure. Having a plan to handle naysayers is just as important to know what you'll do when you have urges. Make sure you know what to say or do when negative comments arise.

CHAPTER FIVE

A NEW YEAR'S PROBLEM

What's something you get asked every New Year? What's your New Year's resolution? For the first few weeks of the year, every person you see will ask you the same thing. It's expected of everybody to make a New Year's resolution, yet they don't work for people. At least not the way people use them.

There's a saying that the definition of insanity is doing the same over and over and again expecting a different result. Then why do people continue to try to make and keep a resolution? People think that resolutions will help them to break some of their bad habits. First, let's look at why a resolution does not work.

1. You're setting the wrong goals.

The most common resolution is to lose weight or get in shape. You wake up the first of January, hop out of bed and say, "I'm going lose 50 pounds this year." By the 15th of January, when you're supposed to be at the gym, you're watching reruns of "The Big Bang Theory" while eating a pint of rocky road. You did nothing wrong. Keeping goals takes more thought than just stating them. These types of goals have little to no leeway. When something happens, and you fail, you will be less likely to make more in the future.

2. Your resolution rarely has to do with the real problem.

You decide to run out and get that gym membership on January first. Good luck fighting the crowd. The gym is going to be packed with everybody else just like you. Once you're in there, you start comparing yourself to everybody. It will definitely help you work through deep-seated psychological issues with inadequacy, rejection, competitiveness and insecurity, but it won't help you solve the real problem. If your goal is to be healthier, then the gym might help, but if you have a problem overeating then it's not going to help. More than likely you're still coming home and eating all the calories you burned off earlier.

3. You set too many.

When making a New Year's resolution a lot of people will think, "While I'm changing this I'll go ahead a change this." Their list of resolutions ends up looking like this;

- Be a better person

- Lose weight

- Sleep more

- Learn a new language

- Drink less

And so on. I get stressed just looking at the list. Our body, as it is, is in homeostasis. It's happy and doesn't want to be changed. The brain has only a finite amount of willpower, and if you start trying to change too many things at once, the brain becomes overwhelmed. The first two weeks of keeping your 10 resolutions may go well, but then your brain starts to smoke and eventually just stops. Then you fall back into old habits.

4. They're too vague.

Let's look at the list above again.

- Be a better person

- Lose weight

- Sleep more

- Learn a new language

- Drink less

They all have something in common. They're about as clear as muddy water. There is no definite way to know if you passed or failed. It's like you teacher gave you an okay on your report card instead of an A or B.

- I want to learn a new language- Great, but what language? Are you trying to learn all languages or a specific one? How are you going to learn your new language? You have no definite plan on how to learn that mysterious new language.

- I want to lose weight- Alright, but how much? Are you overweight and you want to get to a healthier BMI? Do you just want to lose an extra five pounds to fit back into that old dress? You approach those options in very different ways. You have to know how much and why you want to lose weight.

- I want to be a better person- That's admirable, but how? How do you want to be a better person? Do you have a bad temper? Do you use your phone too much? In what way to you want to change? It's great you want to be a better person, but you have to know what aspect of you that you need to change to achieve that goal.

With this new information as to why New Year's

resolutions have a tendency to fail, we can now discover how to make them work. No need to swear them off, instead learn how to make them so that you will actually keep them.

1. Be the person you want to be.

The key to keeping any goal is to imagine that you have already achieved your goal. Don't just say, "I'm going to lose weight," or, "I'm going to stop smoking." Be that person. Visualize you eating healthier and working out regularly. Everybody knows the saying "fake it till you make it," this is the same concept. The more you believe on the inside you are already there, the more it will show on the outside.

2. Make them simple.

In fact make them so stupid simple that completing one seems too easy. Remember the acronym KISS, keep it simple stupid. The simpler the goal is, the easier it is to tell that you have accomplished something.

- If you want to drink less hold yourself to drinking one less drink each day, or each week. Then the next week cut out another drink. Continue doing just that, each week, until you reach your overall goal. You'll know you're achieving your goal when you drink less this week than you did the last.

- If you want to sleep more, start setting the alarm to go to bed. If you typically go to bed at midnight, set the alarm on your phone to go off at 10:30 telling you to get ready for bed. That way you will be in bed by eleven. You'll start waking up more refreshed, and you will quickly see that you're achieving your goals.

- If you want to lose weight set your goal to eat more fruits and vegetables each week. Instead of have French fries with your burger have carrot sticks. Start switching out the high-fat sides with whole veggies. You will start seeing a significant change, and you will know you're achieving your goals.

3. Make yourself more accountable.

When people set a resolution, there's nothing that happens to them if they fail, besides the fact that they don't achieve their goal. Instead of having an easy way out, make it painful to not succeed. Dietbet.com is a website that will help you do just that. They have helped over 150,000 people achieve their weight loss goals. The way it works is you choose one of their plans, which you have to pay for. If you achieve your goal, you will win a part of the pot, the money you put in plus some. If you don't achieve your goal, you get nothing. Of course, you don't need their website to do the same thing. If your goal is to quit smoking tell everybody that if you smoke a cigarette, you will pay x amount of dollars to an acquaintance/co-worker/charity that you don't like. Not only are you giving to something or someone you don't like, but you are also spending money that you could use for something you want or need.

4. Keep the number down.

You probably have a million things you want to change, but you have to narrow down your resolution. As I mentioned before your brain only has a finite amount of change willpower. If you deplete it, then you won't achieve anything. Instead make one very simple goal, which is easy to track, and achieve that first. Once you have achieved that goal, and are confident you created a new habit, then start working on another goal.

New Year's resolutions can either help you or hurt you in your habit breaking goal. You have to be extremely careful in the execution. They can be a good way to help you achieve your goals.

CHAPTER SIX

HABIT FORMING

Bad habits. Now we're going to move into a different direction. It's easier, when trying to break a bad habit, to transform it into a good habit. Not only are you eliminating something wrong, you're also forming something good. It's a win-win. Aristotle said, "We are what we repeatedly do. Excellence then is not an act, but a habit." When you were a child learning how to tie your shoes, you had to repeatedly practice over and over again before you learned how. Now you tie your shoes without even thinking. The same goes for forming a new healthy habit.

There are a lot of programs out there that say if you do something for 21 days it will be stuck in your brain. That's true to an extent. Chances are if you have successfully done your goal for 21 days in a row; you will continue to do it. But like all things, it doesn't necessarily work for everybody or every goal. Fulfilling your goal for 21 days is a huge step in the right direction as long as you remember that you still have to actively work to maintain it.

The Three R's

I spoke earlier about the three step structure of

forming a habit. You can develop a new habit using that same knowledge. The three R's are; reminder, routine, reward. 'Reminder' is the trigger for your habit. Routine is the habit itself. 'Reward' is the positive thing that makes your brain want to continue to repeat the habit.

Step one is to set a reminder for your new habit. You definitely do need motivation to start a new habit, but motivation isn't enough. And it's definitely not the only way. You have to remember to do your new habit. There are several ways to remind yourself to do something. It could simply be putting your workout clothes someplace where you will see them as soon as you wake up. Set the alarm on your phone telling you to eat a healthy lunch. No matter what it is that you want to start doing, you have to remember to do it.

Picking the right reminder is key, though. The best way I know to figure out when to set a reminder is to make a couple of lists. On the first list write down everything you do every day without fail. For example; brushing your teeth, eating breakfast, going to work, turn off lights, go to bed, and so on. Those are all good things you already do that can remind you to perform your new habit. Such as, after I eat breakfast, I'll go for a walk.

On the second list write down everything that happens to you every day. For example; you stop at a stop sign, you hear your favorite song, a commercial comes on, and you get a text. With both of this list you have a wide array of things that you already respond to that you can use as a reminder. If you want to start moving more, every time you hear your favorite song, dance to it. Don't do this if you're driving, though.

Step two is to create a habit that is super easy to start. There are lots of shows on TV showing people shedding lots of weight in a short amount of time. Or you see the runners or swimmers at the Olympics. It makes you want to achieve the same thing. Everybody has those moments where you think you can be just like them. The enthusiasm is great, but it's important to know that lasting changes are a product of habit. Remember, in the words of Leo Babauta, "Make it so easy that you can't say no." At first, performance doesn't matter. The only thing that matters is you strive to do something. Don't worry about how long you run, or how many veggies you eat, it just matters that you are running or eating vegetables. First, decide what you want your new habit to be. Then ask yourself, "How can I make this so easy that I can't say no?"

Step three is to create a reward. You have to celebrate. Celebration is an important part of life. You want to continue to do something that makes you feel good. Since you have to repeat an action for it to become a habit you have to find a way to reward yourself for doing it. If your goal is to exercise, then every time you finish a work out tell yourself, "Good job," or, "Today was a great day." You can also choose to say "Victory" or "Success" every time you practice the new habit. Give yourself credit no matter how big or small the success was.

Step by Step

That's an easy way to start adopting a new healthy habit. Some habits are going to be harder than others to adopt. Here are few other tips to help adopt a new habit.

Make the habit daily. New habits that you only do every few days are harder to adopt. If you want to start exercising, make sure you exercise once a day for the first 30 days. After the first 30 days, you can step down to three or four times a week.

Write down your goal. When you write out, with pen and paper, what you want your goal to be, it will make it seem more important. It makes your idea more real when you write it down.

Make it so you can't lose. Tell yourself you're running an experiment. You're running an experiment for 30 days by doing this new habit. Experiments can't fail. It makes it seem a lot less stressful. Nothing matters until after the first 30 days, and by that time you have adopted your new habit.

A big downfall of people adopting a new habit is that they doubt there self. When you first start working out you may have the thought, "I can't do this as well as they can." Whenever that thought pops into your head add, "But if I continue to work out I will get better at it." You can use this technique with anything.

Know what could happen. Be sure you know all the consequences of not starting your new habit, and know the impact of starting your new habit. Suppose your goal is eating healthier. If you don't start eating healthier, you could start gaining weight and develop health problems. If you do start eating healthier, you will lose weight and have more energy during the day.

Do it for yourself. Don't bog yourself down with the thoughts of what you should do. Instead, focus on what you want to do. You're making these changes for yourself and not for anybody else. Work towards things that motivate you and make your life better. Don't think you have to live your life like everybody around you does.

Switch Bad for Good

One of the best ways to break a bad habit is to switch it out for a good one. It helps to trick your brain and contributes to reduce cravings.

- As always, you have to first identify your triggers. You cannot break bad habits until you figure out what triggers them.

- For every trigger identify a good habit that you could do instead. Instead of smoking when you wake up, what are you going to do? Good habits could be; exercise, meditation, decluttering, organizing, and more.

- For, at least a month, be consistent with those triggers. Every time a trigger comes up act on the good habit you decided to do. The more consistent you are, the more the new habit will become ingrained, and the less you will think of the bad habit.

- Avoid severe trigger situations. You can't always switch out all triggers for new habits. As mentioned before, you might want to skip going out with friends after work for a little while. At least until you get a handle on controlling your urges.

- Discover ways to fight the strong urges. Even though the goal is to switch out the bad habit for a good habit, you will still get the urge to do the bad habit. You will likely need a backup plan when fighting urges.

- Find supportive help. Have somebody you can talk to if things get really rough. Some bad habits are tougher to break than others, and you will go through some tough times, so having somebody you can talk to will help you work through the tough times.

- Stay positive. There will be times when negative thoughts pop into your head. You will have self-sabotaging moments. But the key is to stay positive. When negative thoughts come up, remind yourself why you're doing this.

Remind yourself that you're changing yourself

for the better.

CHAPTER SEVEN

BE SUPPORTIVE

The human mind has the amazing ability to be able to talk you out of doing what you know is right. It can come up with crazy reasons why you shouldn't do something that you know you need to do. You want to work out, "Why? It will make you sweaty." You want to quit smoking, "You'll feel more stress if you do." You want to go to be earlier, "But then you'll miss Jimmy Kimmel." See what I mean. You have to find a way to tell your brain to shut up, and an accountability partner will help you do just that.

Growing up you probably had friends that you would vent to, and they would help you feel better about a situation. An accountability partner works much in the same way.

It will probably feel foreign or uncomfortable the first time. That's a good thing. The uncomfortable feeling is your brain resisting the change. Embrace those feelings. It will be worth it once you work through them.

The role of an accountability partner is to keep you accountable. They help as an outside force to tell your brain to shut up. Their only purpose is to keep you on track. They are there for you when you feel like straying from your path. They're there for you when you wake up in the middle of the night wanting a cupcake. Or when you are extremely stressed out, and you want a cigarette.

Your partner can be anybody that you resonate with. There is no need to pay a professional. They could be a family member, co-worker, friend, or somebody else that is trying to achieve the same goal. Find someone that you connect with and trust to hold you accountable. Be completely open about your goal. What you want to achieve and when you want to achieve it. They are there to be your cheerleader and to hold you to your commitment. Here are some things to look for in choosing your accountability partner:

1. They're reliable. They are easily reached whenever wherever.

2. They want to be your partner. You can't make somebody help you, so make sure they actually want to.

3. Make sure they can relate to you in some way. You don't want to pick someone that has never tried to lose weight to help you lose weight. They won't understand what you're going through.

4. You feel comfortable being honest and open with them, and they are comfortable giving you honest feedback.

Now that you know how to pick your accountability partner, let's talk about the benefits they will provide you. One of the biggest benefits to having an accountability partner is they will accelerate your performance. When you connect with someone one-on-one, you are able to work through the problems of your plan with them. You'll be able to make a sure fire plan to achieve your goals.

Your partner will help you measure your achievements. A good partner will help you to set milestones to reach along the way. It will be easier for you to keep track of your success, and keep you from becoming discouraged. Their outside eyes will see your success more easily than you will be able to.

They will help to validate your thoughts and ideas. Having someone to bounce your ideas off of, besides yourself, will help you to make decisions. They can give you honest outside information. They will help to silence your inner critic.

They help to keep you engaged. Things will come up that will try to distract you from your goals, and you will have someone there to help you stay the path. When you're bored, they will be there for you to talk to. Just knowing that you have somebody there for you will help you to keep your eye on the prize.

Ultimately they will hold you responsible. They are there behind you, pushing you towards your goals. They keep you from getting distracted and hold you accountable. Having a weekly check in with someone, and knowing you have to tell them what you have done this week to achieve your goal, will make you more likely to stay proactive. They keep you from making excuses, and, instead, make deliberate actions towards your end goal.

This isn't to say that you can't achieve your goals by yourself. There are people out there that can, but it takes a lot more willpower. Having a support system will make all the difference in the world.

CHAPTER EIGHT

BOOST YOUR POWER

And that's willpower. Willpower is probably one of the last things you need to work on though. If you don't know what you're trying to change, or why you're doing it, then willpower isn't going to help. You could have great willpower, but without a purpose it's going to fall flat. It's like building a house. You can have all the wood you need, but if you don't have the nails, it's not going to stay together. Once you have your plan in place, then you can move onto willpower.

Willpower and self-control are imperative building blocks for a happy and prosperous life. Some of the most persuasive evidence comes from these two studies.

The first is the marshmallow experiment. Psychologist Walter Mischel started the experiment in the 1960s. He would offer four-year-olds a choice of a marshmallow now or two marshmallows if they could wait 15 minutes. He and his associates then tracked those students as they grew up. They found that the children who were willing to wait 15 minutes for the marshmallows achieved greater academic success, better health, and a less likely chance of divorce.

In the second study, 1,000 children were studied from birth to 32. Researchers found that the children's self-control could predict the future of their health, substance dependence, criminal offenses, and personal finances. It was even true when they eliminated factors such as intelligence and social class.

Use it or lose it

Everybody knows these two factors about muscles:

- Muscles get stronger when exercised

- Muscles can be overworked, which leaves them weak until they have time to rest

But here are some interesting things you may not know.

- In a study, some participants were told not to think about a white bear. Thought-suppression takes a good deal of self-control, especially when told not to think about something. After that, they were told to limit their intake of beer during a taste test because there would be a driving test later. The thought-suppression participants drank more than the non-thought-suppression participants.

- In another study, participants that were asked to suppress their emotions during an upsetting movie gave up sooner during a physical stamina test than those who were freely allowed to express their emotions.

- In a third study, women watched a documentary while seated near a candy bowl. In some, the candy bowl was right next to the woman, in others the candy bowl was across the room from them. Later, they were given hard puzzles to solve. Those that had been seated close to the candy bowl gave up sooner than those who weren't.

In each of these studies, the people that were forced to overuse their willpower or self-control could not fully finish subsequent tasks. Their willpower had been depleted. Now let's look at some ways to strengthen your willpower.

1. Don't keep your willpower depleted

If you have plans to help your friend move heavy pieces of furniture, you're not going to spend 30 minutes before lifting weights. You know your energy will be depleted before you help your friend. The same goes for your willpower. Exercising self-control is an excellent way to build willpower, never giving yourself a break is a good way to deplete it.

2. Meditation

Meditation seems to come up a lot when looking for ways to change habits. It is a great way to strengthen your ability to control your thoughts. But what is meditation? Meditation is simply the practice of bringing your thoughts to the present moment. 47% of lives are spent either thinking about the past, or what has to be done in the future. Leaving us with very little time to think about what we are doing at this present moment. Our brains are very undisciplined. They like to wander. With 10 minutes of meditation each day it will help strengthen your mind and help keep it from wandering. Studies have shown after just 2 to 3 days of 10-minute meditation your brain will be able to focus better, you will have more energy and a lot less stress.

3. Use your imagination

Imagination is an amazing way to improve willpower. The body can respond the same way to an imaginary scenario as the real one. If you imagine laying on a beach, listening to the waves crash, your body will respond by relaxing. On the other hand, if you think about going to work and having a meeting with your boss, your body will tense in response. Dieters are in a constant state of depletion. As a result, they feel everything more intensely. Imagination is able to help control these irritations

In a study, participants were asked to watch a movie with a bowl of chocolate placed nearby. One group was told to imagine they had decided to eat as much as they want. The second group was told to imagine they had eaten none. The third group was told to imagine they had decided to eat the chocolate later. The first group ate more than the other two. Then when given the opportunity to eat later, those that had imagined they would eat later, ate less than the others. They even reported a lesser desire to consume the candy.

4. Use your opposite hand

Researchers have conducted studies that tested corrective actions. One they found that worked particularly well was to use your opposite hand. Your brain is wired to use your dominant hand so it will take willpower to use the non-dominate hand. To practice this, choose a time during the day to use your non-dominate hand. I would suggest doing no more than an hour at a time. More than an hour may deplete your willpower

5. Distract yourself

It's even possible to use your imagination to distract yourself from unwanted thoughts. Just like in the study mentioned earlier about the white bear. When you tell yourself not to think about something, it's going to continually pop back into your head. Train yourself to think about something else. If you don't want to think about that white bear, or cigarettes, or candy, flip your thoughts to something else. Instead of a white bear, think of a black bear. Instead of cigarettes, think of chewing gum. Instead of candy, think of fruit. That puts you in complete control of your thoughts

6. Control your stress

I have mentioned stress several times throughout this book. Stress is the main culprit of many problems. When you become stressed, you'll tend to fall back into old habits. Most of the time you won't even realize it because your body goes into autopilot. When you're stressed, your body releases stress hormones, mainly cortisol.

Cortisol increases your cravings for carbohydrates. Carbs will lower your cortisol levels. Which is probably perhaps why you turn to your friends Ben and Jerry. Alcohol is also a depressant that reduces your cortisol levels. Both of those options hold some negative side effect and aren't helping you to kick those bad habits.

Fortunately, we know these things so you can have control over what you do. The stress response is the same as the fight or flight response, so anything that counterattacks that response will do. Start responding to those stressors by listening to calming music, visualizing calming scenes, or moderate exercise. Whatever works for you. Researchers also say viewing funny videos can help counteract willpower depletion.

The more you practice these habits, the more likely they will be there to help you when major stressors arise.

7. A step at a time

Most of the time people give up on goals, not because of the lack of willpower, but because of feeling overwhelmed in what they are trying to accomplish. I have mentioned something similar to this before. Break your goals down into manageable pieces. That way you can see each step you take instead of trying to consume the whole thing. This also keeps you from depleting your willpower, keeping you recharged and ready to continue working at all times.

8. Be yourself

It takes a lot of effort to suppress you typical behaviors, personality, and preferences. Not surprisingly, it also depletes willpower. Psychologist Mark Muraven found that people who exert self-control to make others happy were more easily depleted than individuals who held true to their own goals and happiness. People pleasures may find they are at a disadvantage when it comes to willpower as opposed to those who are secure and comfortable with their self.

9. Change your speech

In another correction study, researchers conducted to modify the subject's natural speech. This would include resisting the urge to say a cuss word, or simply change from saying "hey" to "hello." It takes willpower to make the conscious effort to change one's speech, especially when we typically speak out of instinct. It doesn't matter what you do to change your speech, as long as you make a conscious effort to switch things up. Just like using your opposite hand, choose a chunk of your day where you will change the way you speak. You also need to decide what it is that you are going to change. You might choose to stop swearing, or to stop saying slang words like "ain't." Remember to only practice this for about an hour at a time, or you may deplete your willpower. After only two weeks you will see an increase in your willpower.

10. Keep temptations at bay

With most habits, you have a weakness for what you like to consume. If you drink too much keep alcohol out of your house. If you smoke, get rid of all your cigarettes. If you snack a lot, either get rid of the junk food or put it out of sight. There will be times when you see your weakness, and you will need to make a plan for that moment. Decide how you are going to handle it. If your weakness is junk food and you have children, chances are junk food is going to enter your house at some point. No matter where the kids got the food, grandma, trick or treating, school, work out a plan where you don't constantly see it. Work with your spouse or significant other. Have them take all the junk food and put it where you don't know where it is. If the kids want some, they have to ask the other parent, not you. And you have to promise that you won't beg and plead to know where it is. That takes a little willpower in itself, but a lot less than trying to keep from eating the junk food that you see.

Willpower is just like any other muscle in your body. With the right practice, it can be strengthened. I have just given you 10 ways to increase your willpower and self-control, but don't try to do all 10 at once. You'll just end up driving yourself crazy. Think of training your willpower just like you would prepare for a race. On your first day of training, you're not going to run the full 26 miles. Not unless you're already an Olympic runner. Instead, you will increase the amount you run every day. Choose one of these to start using on a daily basis. Once you feel that's not working for you anymore, pick a different one. Before you know it, you will be more mentally strong.

CHAPTER NINE

MEDITATIVE STATE

Mediation has proved to be very helpful in most aspects of life. It has shown up numerous times already in this book. Since it seems to be so useful, I figured I would dedicate a whole chapter to it. We'll take a deeper look into the benefits of meditation and how it will help you break your bad habits. Then I will give you a simple step by step on how to get started meditating for beginners. If you already meditate, then you have a leg up.

Ask anybody that meditates, and they will tell you it's good for you. But in what way? Is that just from years of practice, or is there scientific research out there that proves it's good for you? Here are some general ways that mediation can help:

- Improves willpower

- Improves focus

- Decreases stress

- Improves ability to learn

- Increases energy

There are over 3,000 scientific studies that examine the benefits of meditation. I'm going to summarize some of the findings for you.

- Decreases depression

In Belgium, a study was conducted at five middle schools involving approximately 400 students. Professor Filip Raes concluded that the students that participated in mindfulness meditation reduced indication of anxiety, stress, and depression for up to six months later. At the University of California, a similar study was conducted with formerly depressive patients and concluded that mindfulness meditation reduced ruminative thinking and dysfunctional beliefs.

- Reduces panic disorder

The American Journal of Psychiatry published a study where 22 patients diagnosed with panic disorder were submitted to 3 months of meditation and relaxation training. 20 of the 22 participants showed that their panic and anxiety had been reduced significantly, and the changes were maintained at follow-up.

- Increases concentration

Harvard neuroscientists ran an experiment where 16 people took part in an 8-week mindfulness course. They used guided meditation and integration of mindfulness in everyday activities. Sara Lazer, Ph.D., reported at the end, MRI scans showed that gray matter concentration increased in areas of the brain involved in learning, memory, emotion regulation, sense of self, and perspective.

- Increases focus in spite of distraction

Emory University did a study that demonstrated that participants with more mediation experience exhibited increased connectivity within the brain controlling attention. The neural relationships may be involved in the development of cognitive skills.

- Prevents you from falling in a multitasking trap

Multitasking is a dangerous productivity myth that will deplete you of energy and is a source of stress. Switching between tasks is costly to your brain which can cause feelings of distraction and dissatisfaction. In a study conducted by the University of Washington and the University of Arizona, human resources personnel took part in 8 weeks of in either mindfulness meditation or body relaxation techniques. They were given stressful multitasking tests before and after training. Groups that had practice meditation showed lower stress levels and a better recall of the tasks they had done. They also switched between tasks less often, concentrating on one task for a longer amount of time.

- Increases unconscious mind awareness

A study done by the University of Sussex found that people who practiced mindfulness meditation experienced a longer paused between unconscious impulses and action. They were also less susceptible to hypnosis.

- Reduces heart diseases and stroke

Cardiovascular disease kills more people in the world than anything else. A study performed in 2012, studied 200 high-risk individuals. They were asked to, either, take part in a health education class promoting better diet and exercise, or take a class on transcendental meditation. During the next five years, they found that those who took the meditation class decreased their overall risk of heart disease, stroke, and death by 48%.

- Increases compassion and decreases worry

After 9 weeks of compassion cultivation training, participants showed significant improvement in all three domains of compassion (compassion for others, receiving compassion, and self-compassion).

- Decreases emotional eating

Scientists have found that transcendental meditation decreases the likelihood of emotional eating, which helps to prevent obesity.

There is a lot more scientific information out there that proves meditation can help with all aspects of life. It's no wonder that it shows up a lot in contributing to quit bad habits.

Simple meditation practice

If you've never meditated before, I would suggest doing a guided meditation. A quick search on the internet will turn up several apps and downloads for guided meditation. Some free choices are Omvana, Headspace, Calm, Smiling Mind, and Take a Break.

If you want to meditate on your own here is a simple meditation practice designed by Headspace App founder, Andy Puddicombe:

1. Find a quiet room where you can sit comfortably upright with no distraction.

2. Set a 10-minute timer, and get comfortable in your chair.

3. Find something in your line of vision to focus on for 6 deep breaths. With each exhale, allow your body to soften as you become more relaxed. On the 6th exhale, close your eyes.

4. Focus your attention on the points of contact between your body and the chair and floor. Notice the sensation of your arms, back, and bottom on the chair, and your feet on the floor.

5. Then become aware of your surroundings. Notice all the sounds and smells around you.

Anything that you can sense without your sight.

6. Then focus on your breath. Notice how your chest expands when you breathe in and how it contracts when you exhale.

7. Once you're comfortable with the rhythm of your breathing, begin to count. 1 on the inhale, 2 on the exhale, all the way up to 10. This will keep your mind focused on your breath and keep it from wandering.

8. When you make it to 10, start back over at 1. Do not count 11, 12, 13, etc.

9. While you breathe, allow your thoughts to come and go. You can't stop yourself from thinking. What you want to do is avoid lingering on one thought. The moment you realize your mind has wandered, bring it back to your breaths.

10. Continue until your timer goes off.

The first time you do this, it will probably seem awkward and weird. It's just like adopting a new habit. The more you do it, the less uncomfortable it becomes, and the easier it will be to do.

Here are some other, more advanced, mediation options:

- Candle starting

If you have problems focusing, you can light a candle and stare at it. Make sure the candle is at eye level. If you find your mind wandering, return your focus to what the flame is doing. Another level up is to stare at the candle without blinking. It will eventually make you cry which refreshes your eyes.

- Mantra

The repetition of words helps you to find calm and focus. You can find different mantras online, or you can make up your own. It doesn't matter what you say as long as it resonates with you, and you're happy with it.

- Visualization

Another fun and easy way to meditate is to visualize an idyllic being or setting in your mind. You can make it whatever you want. Embellishing it as much or as little as you need.

- Become the Observer

Become the observer of your mind. Close your eyes and focus on the spot, about an inch, above the spot between your eyebrows, third eye chakra. Begin to focus on what you mind and body is feeling, thinking and doing.

You should now be able to use meditation to help you break your bad habits, and, in the process, start a new good, habit.

I'm sure you are dying to start working on getting rid of that bad habit that's been bothering you, so I'll wrap this up. Remember to keep this simple. Don't overwhelm yourself with too many goals, or trying too many of these techniques at once. Be prepared to fail and meet naysayers, they are inevitable, but you don't have to let them control you. If nothing else, please remember you deserve to live the best life possible.

CONCLUSION

I hope this book was able to help you to break your bad habits, and adopt new, healthy habits.The next step is to start implementing the new things you have learned and start seeing the change within yourself. You deserve to live your best life possible.

THANK YOU

Dear treasured reader, I would like to thank you from the bottom of my heart purchasing this valuable resource on transforming your habits. I sincerely hope the book is able to help you realize your dream of living the life you were meant to live.

I hope you've gotten some valuable information that you can use daily to better your life and those around you as well. If you liked it would you be so kind as to leave an honest/positive review for my book. I would appreciate it very much.

Here's to your financially free, rewarding and profitable life.

To Your Success,

John S. Lawson